The Library of
NATIVE AMERICANS™

The Mojave
of California and Arizona

Jack S. Williams

The Rosen Publishing Group's
PowerKids Press™
New York

For Robert Hoover, who taught me that caring about students
was perhaps the most important lesson of all

Published in 2004 by The Rosen Publishing Group, Inc.
29 East 21st Street, New York, NY 10010

Photo and illustration credits: cover, pp. 12 (#3418), 16 (#1241), 23 (#1908), 24 (#3424), 26 (#3980), 28 (#1402) courtesy of University of Southern California, on behalf of the USC Specialized Libraries and Archival Collections; p. 4 © David Muench/Corbis; pp. 6–7 © National Geographic Image Collection; p. 8 © Royalty Free/Corbis; p. 10 © AP Photo/*Yuma Daily Sun*, Paul M. Perez; pp. 14, 31, 42 Print Collection, Miriam and Ira D. Wallach Division of Art, Prints, and Photographs, New York Public Library Astor, Lenox, and Tilden Foundations; pp. 19 (X-32566), 30 (X-32568) Western History Collection/Denver Public Library; pp. 22, 35 National Anthropological Archives, Smithsonian Institution, INV#06429900, INV#09006701; p. 25 © Harvey Spector Photography; p. 33 © Corbis; p. 34 courtesy of the Oakland Museum of California; pp. 36, 44, 46 © Hulton/Archive/Getty Images; pp. 38, 40 Library of Congress, Prints and Photographs Division; p. 47 courtesy of the Seaver Center for Western History Research, Natural History Museum of Los Angeles; pp. 48, 52, 54 National Archives and Records Administration; pp. 49, 50, 51 courtesy of The Bancroft Library, University of California, Berkeley; p. 56 © AP Photo/Rhonda Birndorf.

Book Design: Geri Fletcher; Editor: Charles Hofer; Photo Researcher: Sherri Liberman

Williams, Jack S.
The Mojave of California and Arizona / Jack S. Williams.— 1st ed.
      p. cm. — (The library of Native Americans)
Summary: Describes the origins, history, politics, and culture of the Mojave people of the desert southwest, from prehistory to the present. Includes bibliographical references and index.
ISBN 1-4042-2661-3 (lib. bdg.)
1. Mohave Indians—History—Juvenile literature. 2. Mohave Indians—Social life and customs—Juvenile literature. [1. Mohave Indians. 2. Indians of North America—California. 3. Indians of North America—Arizona.] I. Title. II. Series.
E99.M77W55 2004
979.1004'975722
                                                                                        2003015649

Manufactured in the United States of America

On the cover: Mojave beadwork.

A variety of terminologies has been employed in works about Native Americans. There are sometimes differences between the original names or terms used by a Native American group and the anglicized or modernized versions of such names or terms. Although this book contains terms that we feel will be most recognizable to our readership, there may also exist synonymous or native words that are preferred by certain speakers.

Contents

One

Introducing the Mojave People

The waters of the powerful Colorado River traverse one of the driest, flattest parts of the North American continent. It is hard to imagine what the first European explorers thought when they sailed up the river from Mexico in 1540. As they went north, they passed scorched deserts and rocky mountains. Finally, the waters grew shallower, and the seafarers had to turn around. When they returned to Mexico, they gave a fantastic description of the places they had visited. The bright blue sky seemed to be held in place by giant colored stacks of exposed rock. The land had mysterious inhabitants who waved at them from the shore. This was the first encounter between Europeans and the Mojave.

The word "Mojave" (pronounced mo-HA-vey) comes from a Native American name for a group of three mountains located near the modern town of Needles, California. The Mojave called the place hamakhava. When Spaniards heard this word, they thought it sounded like "Mojave." When Anglo-Americans adopted the name, they changed the "j" to an "h," so that the spelling would follow English pronunciation rules. The members of the Mojave Nation call themselves the Pipa Aha Macav. This term means "people who live along the water."

The Colorado River was an important part of Mojave culture. The river's rich resources would allow the Mojave to develop farming practices.

6   This illustration shows what life may have been like for the very first inhabitants of North America. These people crossed the land bridge that once connected North America and Asia.

The Mojave are the northernmost Yuman-speaking tribe. When Europeans first met them, they were divided into three major groups. The northern Mathalyathum lived from the Black Canyon to the Mojave Valley. The Huttonpah lived on the central segment of the river. The southern Kavilyathum lived in an area that stretched from the southern end of the Mojave Valley to a place just south of Needles Peak. Today, these lands include parts of Arizona, California, and Nevada. By 1540, there were probably about 3,000 to 4,000 Mojave.

The Mojave Nation learned to live in one of the harshest desert regions on Earth. Since 1540, they have overcome a series of dramatic challenges that were created by outsiders.

ARIZONA

The Mojave
Territory

NEVADA

CALIFORNIA

Nevada

Area of
Detail

California

Despite many setbacks, the Mojave have survived and even learned to prosper. Today they stand as an example of Native American determination to preserve their heritage.

Some Mojave believe that they have always lived in the area where they live today. Most scholars think that they moved to the Colorado River area thousands of years ago, along with the other Yuman-language speakers, including their neighbors, the Quechan, the Kamia, the Kumeyaay, and the Halchidhoma. No one kept written records during this ancient period. Researchers are still trying to determine where the Mojave people came from and when they arrived in the southwestern part of North America.

The scholars who study the objects left behind by the earliest Native Americans are called archaeologists. Other experts, known as linguistic anthropologists, study the ways that languages come into being and change over long periods of time. Although these experts have had to make a lot of guesses, they have put together a general picture of the beginnings and awesome journeys of the Mojave Nation.

The first people to live in North America entered the continent sometime between 13,000 and 40,000 years ago. Their ancestors came from eastern Asia using a bridge made up of ice and small rocky islands. The first Native Americans probably followed herds of wild animals, which they hunted as a source of food. As the centuries passed, the Mojave's ancestors moved south. Finally, they came to a warmer region, with many different food resources. Within less than a thousand years, the Native Americans spread over both North America and South America.

This map details the Mojave's territory.

10 The Colorado River flows lazily through the Mojave territory near Yuma, Arizona. For thousands of years, the Mojave have built their villages along the banks of the river.

The mountains and valleys that the ancient travelers saw are the same that we can see today. The climate during this early era was extremely different. Areas that are now very dry and hot were cooler and wetter. The lower parts of the Southwest had beautiful clear lakes, rolling grasslands, and dense forests. It was probably during this period that the Mojave first built houses along the shores of the Colorado River. For thousands of years, they made their living by hunting and gathering.

By the year AD 1, the climate had dramatically changed. For a long time, the people had survived by improving their skills as hunters and gatherers. Also around this time, several new ideas began reaching the Mojave from the south. For many centuries the Native Americans of central Mexico had been living as food producers. The Mojave learned that they could grow corn, beans, and squash, along with many other plants. They also learned the secrets of making pottery. The people of the Colorado River soon combined their older ways with the new ideas.

Two

Daily Life

The Spanish explorers were amazed by the people they found living along the Colorado River. It was hard to believe that anyone could survive in such a fiery place. The newcomers eventually learned that the Mojave were excellent farmers and tough warriors. They had their own unique religion, clothes, tools, jewelry, and houses. Very few outsiders have appreciated the amazing skills that made the early Mojave way of life possible.

Living by a Desert River

Two great forces dominated the ancient Mojave's environment. These were the desert and the Colorado River. The banks of the river are thick with reeds and water plants. Every year there were floods that brought a fresh layer of black soil from the north. This rich soil provided a perfect home for many kinds of useful wild plants. It was also ideal for farming.

Beyond the river valley, there are immense barren mountains and dust-coated valleys. The brown landscape is dotted by ancient volcanic cones and timeworn lava flows. Here, the sandy soil was not useful for farming. In contrast with the river valley, the few plants found away from the river valley were thorny and small.

This photo was taken near the turn of the twentieth century. It captures a Mojave woman and child in native dress.

Without the gift of water from the Colorado River, the land is extremely dry. Each year, only 4 to 8 inches (10 to 20 centimeters) of moisture fall from the sky. When miners explored the Mojave's dry desert regions after 1850, they often described them as a living hell. By contrast, the cool waters of the river created an oasis that was almost like paradise.

The climate changes radically during the year. The winters are relatively mild and pleasant. The temperatures rarely rise above 75°F (23°C). During this season, it sometimes rains, but most of the time it is sunny and dry. During the spring, the temperatures

This illustration, done in 1858, depicts a typical Mojave home.

gradually increase, and it rarely rains. By the end of May, the sun climbs into the sky each morning with a blistering vengeance. June is even hotter, with daily average temperatures of more than 105°F (37°C). During the late summer, thunderstorms fill the skies with lightning and rain clouds. The fall season sees small amounts of rain as the temperatures slowly drop.

In order to survive in this harsh climate, the Mojave developed an amazing set of skills that combined farming, gathering, and hunting. More than anything else, it was the Colorado River that was the key to their survival and strength as a people.

Villages

The Mojave lived in small settlements made up of several clusters of houses, spread out over a large area. Their biggest villages rarely included more than fifty people. Some communities had only one or two families. The villages were often moved and reorganized. A person might live in several different settlements during his or her lifetime.

The Mojave houses had a rectangular floor plan. The average structure measured about 20 by 20 feet (6.1 meters) to 25 feet (7.6 m). Community leaders sometimes had homes that were twice this size. These homes were used for meetings and as a shelter for visitors. The walls were made out of logs. Three of the four sides sloped toward the flat roof. This thatch-and-reed covering was held in place by poles. Each home was built inside a deep pit. The exterior was covered by mud and grass. The soil that surrounded the house helped to keep the structure cool during the fierce summer heat. The doorway to the house always faced south. It was the only opening, and it allowed cooking smoke to escape and sunlight to brighten the interior. A mat was used to cover the entranceway. Most houses had a fire pit in the middle of the room that was used for cooking. The floor was covered with fine sand. The people who lived in the house normally slept on mats that were arranged along the walls.

16 Mojave homes, like the one in this photograph, were built to endure the harsh landscape that surrounded them.

The Mojave also built tall, cylindrical storehouses for grain. The walls of these structures were made out of branches that were laced together. The villages also included temporary coverings made from poles, grasses, reeds, and brush. These shelters provided protection against the sun and dusty desert winds.

Farming

The Mojave Nation adopted its basic farming methods from peoples living farther south, in what is today northern Mexico. Their major food crops were corn, beans, and squashes. The Mojave also planted several types of wild edible grasses. After 1780, the Colorado River people adopted wheat and melons. These plants were introduced by the European missionaries.

The Mojave did not use ditches to water their crops. Instead, they planted the seeds in the rich black soil that was deposited along the riverbanks during the summer floods. These same over-flowing waters provided moisture to the plants, along with important minerals and nutrients. The warm temperatures ensured that the crops would grow quickly. The produce was ready to be harvested in the early fall.

Although their farming methods sound simple, the Mojave actually had to work very hard to prepare the land for their crops. Many of the best areas were covered by trees and brush that had to be cut down using dull stone axes or burned off using fire.

Once the land had been cleared, the Mojave could plant their crops. The seeds were scattered in irregular patterns. The main tool used was the digging stick. During the months that followed, the Mojave children carefully guarded the fields from wild animals that loved to eat the seeds and tender young plants. The Mojave also had to pull out any weeds that sprouted near their plants.

Gathering

Although the Mojave's crops were important, the native women and children also spent a great deal of time gathering wild seeds, roots, and other greens. Wild plants made up about half of all the people's meals. The most important resources of this type were probably the mesquite trees that produced wonderful bean pods. Other plants were used as medicines and as raw materials for craft projects.

Hunting and Fishing

Larger animals were relatively rare in the Mojave territory. As a result, these Native Americans did a lot less hunting in their homeland than some of their neighbors. The men sometimes ventured into other nations' territories in search of animals. These areas had bighorn sheep, deer, pronghorn antelope, and many other large mammals. Smaller creatures that were found almost everywhere included rabbits, rats, mice, and birds. The Mojave avoided eating certain kinds of animals, including most reptiles.

The Colorado River was filled with tasty fish. The Mojave used a combination of spears, nets, and basket traps to capture these creatures. They sometimes used boats made from reeds when fishing along the riverbanks.

Cooking

The Mojave women usually prepared the family's meals. They used many different techniques to prepare the food. Their dishes were delicious and extremely nutritious.

Mojave women were mostly responsible for preparing food. This photo, taken in the late 1800s, shows Mojave men and women around a typical Mojave cooking area. Grain storage areas can be seen in the background.

Corn, as well as many types of wild plants, were ground into powder using stone tools. One of the items found in almost every kitchen was a metate. This large, slablike piece of stone was used with a fist-sized piece of rock called a mano. Corn kernels and other kinds of seeds were placed on the surface of the metate. The mano was pushed and rocked back and forth in order to crush the grain. Some seeds and plants were crushed using a long, cylinder-shaped pestle and a bowl-like wooden mortar.

The Mojave cooked many kinds of food over an open flame. They created fires using a special wooden rod that fit into another piece of wood. This device is called a fire drill. In order to start the fire, the rod was rapidly twirled using two hands. Eventually, the friction would cause the smaller piece of the wood to smoke and then flame. The fire was quickly transferred to leaves or dry grass. Pieces of wood could then be added as fuel.

Every Mojave family also owned a set of pottery bowls, jars, and pots. These items were used to cook and store food. The Mojave also traded for baskets that were used for storage.

Native chiefs sometimes baked their dishes in earth or sand ovens or roasting pits. The Native Americans would dig a deep hole in the ground. They would then light a large fire. After several hours, they would use sticks to remove the burning wood. Meat or vegetables were wrapped in leaves or reeds before being placed in the center of the hole. The earth or sand was then placed back in the pit. In a few hours, the food could be removed. It was now ready to eat.

In order to smoke meat and fish, the Mojave would build a fire. The flesh would be cut into long, narrow strips. These items were then placed on a rack or a low branch over the flame. After a few hours, the meat or fish was removed, and it could be stored for later use.

Many of the Mojave dishes were similar to modern stews or porridges. Some vegetables and fruits, such as cactus pads, could be eaten without any additional preparation.

Clothing and Body Decoration

The Mojave lived in a warm, dry climate. As a result, they wore small amounts of clothing. Most men wore small pieces of animal skin, called breechcloths, suspended from their belts. The younger children wore no clothing. Older girls and women wore skirts or aprons. They also put on short skin or fur capes. Both men and women wore sandals made out of cactus fibers.

Nearly all of the Mojave loved tattoos. There were many different styles that combined dots and lines in dozens of patterns. The Mojave also wore jewelry made from wood, bone, and shell. Men and women wore long nose rods. During religious ceremonies, the Mojave decorated their faces and bodies with red and yellow paint.

Mojave men wore their hair long. They would often make braids and wrap them around their heads. The women wore their hair at shoulder length. The front was cut over the eyes to create bangs.

22 Tattoo art was an important part of the Mojave culture. This Mojave man wears facial tattoos for both cosmetic and religious purposes.

Arts and Crafts

The Mojave created many different kinds of tools and beautiful objects for everyday use. Most of these items were crafted using the resources they found around them.

The men were experts at manufacturing stone tools. Most of the items that had to have sharp edges were manufactured by chipping pieces of flint, basalt, and similar rocks. The Mojave tool kit included knives, spearheads, arrowheads, scrapers, and drills. Other types of stone tools were made by grinding rocks together. The Mojave's favorite types of raw materials included basalt and sandstone. Most households had family metates, manos, pestles, and arrow shaft straighteners.

This man is wearing a nose rod, which was common within the Mojave Nation.

The Native American women made baskets, fish traps, drums, and trays out of woven plant fibers. The Mojave also purchased various kinds of similar items from their neighbors. Some clothing, such as belts and skirts, was also made out of plant fibers, although most items were made from animal skins.

The Mojave were excellent pottery makers. They gathered the clay that they needed from the river bottom. The earth was combined with water and crushed sandstone before it was formed into long, cigar-shaped pieces. These pieces were coiled to create vessels. The Mojave's pottery included jars, bowls, ladles, pots, trays, and dishes. The surface of the clay was smoothed using a wooden paddle and a small round stone. Each clay item was carefully dried before it was piled together with fuel and burned to harden. Some types of pottery were painted and then burned for a second time. The red decorations usually had patterns named for animals or plants.

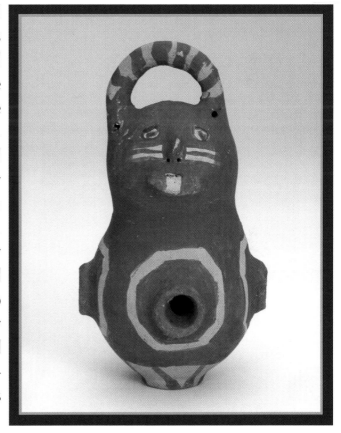

The Mojave were well-known for their pottery, such as this canteen *(above)*. Pottery was made from clay gathered from riverbeds found throughout the Mojave territory. The Mojave used beadwork to create many beautiful designs *(left)* used for clothing.

26 The Mojave were also skilled with other arts and crafts. This Mojave woman is doing beadwork using traditional methods.

The Mojave used many types of wild plants. Some of the vegetation was made into powerful medicines. Other plants were used in religious rituals. Wood was used for digging sticks, mortars, arrows, bows, spears, war clubs, stirring sticks, and house poles. Plants, such as yucca, were made into strong threads or cords. The Mojave also combined bundles of reeds to create rafts. These boats could hold up to five people. They were used in fishing and to cross the Colorado River.

The Mojave depended on the animal world for other important resources. Skins and furs were turned into breechcloths, skirts, capes, bags, belts, ropes, and blankets. Pieces of bone were turned into awls, gaming sticks, hairpins, and needles.

Trade

The Mojave made most of the things they needed. Sometimes the men went on long journeys in order to trade. They traveled all the way from the Pacific coast of southern California to the Gila River O'odham settlements north of Tucson, Arizona. The trading expeditions usually departed with corn, pumpkins, melons, and yellow squash. They returned with items such as animal skins, baskets, jewelry, seashells, wooden bowls, and horn spoons.

Three

Other Aspects of Mojave Life

Membership in different Mojave groups was based on whether or not someone was a man or a woman, his or her age, how much wealth he or she had, and who his or her parents were. The things that were most important to the Mojave's sense of identity were their family, their clan, and their membership in the nation.

The smallest Mojave social unit was the family. The oldest male was responsible for leading this group. Some men were allowed to have more than one wife. Mojave men and women remarried many times. Some men owned women or girl slaves who had to take orders from the family members. Every Mojave family had its own farming and gathering areas. No one else was allowed to use these resources without permission.

The Mojave families were joined together to form twenty-two clans. The members of each group claimed to have had a common ancestor, such as the sun or a rattlesnake. A person joined his or her father's clan when he or she was born. No one was allowed to get married to anyone in his or her own clan.

Most Mojave men believed that they were the equals of everyone else, except for their slaves. A man was given special recognition if he was generous or he defeated many enemies in battle. The village, regional, and overall chiefs were the most

In this photo, taken in the late nineteenth century, many Mojave are gathered to mourn the death of their chief, Sistuma.

honored people in the community. These men were given many gifts by their followers. However, they were expected to distribute these items when their people faced crises, such as droughts, or when there was going to be an important religious celebration. The position of chief was usually handed down from a father to his son. Some political leaders were chosen by the community based on their knowledge and abilities.

This photo shows a Mojave camp and family during the late nineteenth century.

The Mojave had a number of other smaller social groups. The chiefs were helped by special organizers for religious celebrations. There were also generals, who were usually selected on the basis of ability. Some people specialized in religion and healing. They often collected sacred objects and performed rituals that gave them supernatural powers. People feared these individuals because they could use their abilities for evil as well as good.

Government

The Mojave Nation was ruled through a system of political leaders who were given different amounts of power. Every village had a chief. All the villages were combined to form three large districts that were ruled by a single political leader, or super chief. These three regional

The Mojave would adopt many things from the newcomers, including some styles of dress. This portrait of Mojave chief Irétabe, taken in the late nineteenth century, shows him wearing a European-style jacket.

groups combined to form the Mojave Nation. Important decisions were made by the super chief with the most prestige. The leader of the nation worked hard to protect the people's territory from invasion. Anyone who came into the Mojave territory had to get his permission. Although they were important, none of the chiefs had complete, or absolute, power over their subjects. They usually led by example.

Warfare

The Mojave Nation fought as a single force under the control of the senior super chief. The people went to war for a number of different reasons. They almost always defended themselves against invaders. The early Mojave used a combination of bows and arrows and clubs in combat. Many warriors also carried spears and round leather shields.

Sometimes the Mojave fought their neighbors in order to conquer their lands. Other conflicts started when warriors decided to gain recognition by capturing slaves or taking food from neighboring nations.

As newcomers encroached on their land, the Mojave adopted different types of warfare. Here, a Mojave boy poses with a traditional bow and arrow. Laying on the ground is a rifle.

Religion

The Mojave's religion taught them the things they needed to know in order to be good and productive members of their community. Many of their ideas about God focused on their dreams. They believed that a wide variety of supernatural forces communicated with them during their sleep. Throughout people's lives, there were special occasions when their dreams gave them direction.

34 This illustration depicts what the newcomers called a "mystic maze." According to some of the settlers, the Native Americans believed that the souls of the dead wandered through the maze in search of "happy hunting grounds."

The Mojave believed the most important dreams came when boys became men, and girls became women.

Mojave children spent a great deal of time learning religious songs and rituals. These educational sessions included information about history and supernatural beings, as well as the deeds of famous warriors. Community elders used stories to help young people understand their faith. One of the accounts tells about how the earth and sky came together to form the great spirit, Matavilya. He was sadly killed by Frog Woman before he could tell the Mojave how to live. This job then fell to his little brother, Mastambo. At that time, the people of the nation were living in a world without animals, plants, or even land. Mastambo created the creatures of the Mojave world and then taught the native peoples everything they needed to know in order to live well. He even drove a willow into the land and drew out the water that became the Colorado River. Mastambo gave the river and the land that surrounded it to the Mojave.

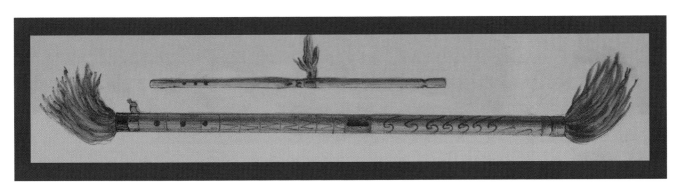

The Mojave made many instruments fashioned from materials found in the natural world around them. This illustration depicts a Mojave fife and flute, probably made from wood and reeds. Instruments like these were probably used in religious ceremonies.

36   Face painting was an important part of Mojave culture. This practice was often employed for religious purposes.

As a Mojave neared death, his or her community would begin a series of special rituals with sad songs and a great deal of crying. After he or she was gone, the body and the dead person's property were burned on a funeral pyre. The people would never speak the name of the person again.

The Mojave sometimes scratched the surface of rock outcroppings with symbols or markings. These designs are called petroglyphs. Other signs were made in the desert surface by turning over rocks. These massive designs could be seen only from the air.

Both kinds of images are sometimes called rock art. It is important that anyone who views these depictions shows respect, as many modern Mojave consider them to be sacred.

Four

Dealing with the Newcomers

Hernando de Alarcón commanded the first European ships to sail up the Colorado River. His vessels reached the general area of the Mojave people around 1540. During the next 200 years, Spanish treasure hunters, soldiers, and missionaries passed through the region. These men included Juan de Oñate (1604–1605), Father Eusebio Kino (1698–1702), and Father Jacobo Sedelmayr (1748). By the last quarter of the eighteenth century, European colonists were living in what is today California and Arizona. Even so, the vast deserts that surrounded the river kept most foreigners away from the Mojave.

But even the desert rocks and sand could not shield the Native Americans from some of the changes that Europeans brought to the Southwest. New diseases, such as measles and smallpox, spread to the interior of the continent with terrifying results. Among some nations, as many as 90 percent of the people were killed. The Mojave probably suffered terrible losses between 1550 and 1700.

The Mojave and the Spanish Empire

After 1750, Spain developed military colonies and missions that were relatively close to the Colorado River. In the west, a series of

This illustration, done in the mid-nineteenth century, captures life along the Colorado River in the Mojave territory. Slowly, European settlers moved into Mojave land, forever changing the natives' way of life.

outposts were built along the California coastline. To the east and south, missions and presidios were built along the rivers of Arizona and Sonora in northern Mexico. It was only a matter of time before the invaders would try to connect the two areas using the old native trail system that crossed the Colorado River. The development of the new route by Europeans led to the creation of two Spanish outposts to the south of the Mojave, among their close military allies, the Quechan. The native people of the Colorado River rebelled and destroyed these settlements less than a year after their founding. For many years, the Mojave were able to prevent foreigners from moving into their lands.

40 This portrait of Hernando de Alarcón was painted in 1791. In 1540, Alarcón became the first European to visit the Mojave territory.

At first it seemed that there might be friendship with the newcomers. In 1771, the Franciscan missionary Francisco Garcés began his work among the Native Americans of the Colorado River. By 1775, he was attempting to teach Christianity to the Mojave, whom he called Jamajabs. That same year, a large group of colonists moved from Arizona to California, following a path that took them through the Quechan country. In 1781, Garcés actually founded two combined missions and towns near Yuma.

The Native Americans soon learned that the foreigners could not be trusted. A large herd of horses and cattle were brought to the Colorado River in the summer of 1781. There had been a terrible drought on the river. Food was scarce. The animals were allowed to eat the Quechan's and Mojave's precious mesquite beans. Although the invaders didn't even realize the plants were important, they had proven themselves to be dangerous and unfriendly guests.

The Mojave and the Quechan burned the missions and towns and killed or captured all of the Spanish colonists. As a result, more Europeans came with a large army. During the next four years, the war continued. Finally, in 1783, the invaders' army departed. The Quechan and the Mojave had won a remarkable victory.

The Colorado River Native Americans did keep some of the things the invaders brought. Horses provided a useful source of food and transportation. They were also valuable in warfare. Glass beads, gained by trade, were beautiful additions to the traditional types of jewelry used by Native Americans. Wheat and several types of melons were also introduced. The Mojave also developed a liking for steel knives, firearms, and European clothing.

During the later Spanish period, there were other changes that took place in the surrounding deserts that affected the Mojave. New types of European diseases killed many native people. Some animals and plants that were brought by the Europeans spread into the interior, destroying many of the old plants that had been used by the Mojave. The old trade networks disappeared and a new kind of commerce began. There had always been a market for slaves on

This illustration, done around 1855, depicts newcomers venturing up the Colorado River in search of new land. Native Americans look on in wonder as these new and strange people arrive.

the Colorado River. Now, some Spanish settlers also offered trade goods for captives. Many Mojave became middlemen in the slave trade. Other warriors used their horses to raid areas as far away as central Nevada and the coastal missions near Los Angeles.

When Mojave warriors hit the coastal outposts, the Spanish army sometimes tried to counterattack. The Spanish troops fought their way to the Colorado River in 1796 and 1819, but they accomplished almost nothing. Time and again, Native Americans ambushed them or escaped into the surrounding desert. The Mojave and the Quechan remained the most important nations on the lower Colorado River.

The Mojave and the Mexican Republic

In 1821, Mexico became independent of Spain. Colonists on the frontier soon developed a plan to reopen the route that linked California to Arizona. In 1823, missionaries from lower California reached Tucson, Arizona. A year later, Santiago Arguëllo, a Mexican officer from San Diego, fought his way to the Colorado River. In 1825, the government in Mexico City ordered troops from California and Arizona to conquer the Quechan and the Mojave. The two armies reached the river when a major revolt broke out among the Yaquis, who lived in northwestern Mexico. The armies had to be called back. The route was not reopened during the Mexican period in California and Arizona. Mojave warriors continued their offensives into the coastal regions through the middle of the nineteenth century.

Around 1825, new foreigners began to explore the Colorado River valley. These men were fur trappers who came in search of beavers. The first man to lead an expedition into the Mojave region was Jedediah Smith. He arrived in 1826 and established friendships with the Native Americans. The next year, a trapper named James Ohio Pattie broke Mojave law by taking beaver skins without paying for permission. A fight broke out in which two newcomers and sixteen Mojave died. When Smith returned later

This painting captures the Battle of Monterrey (Mexico) during the Mexican–American War. As a result of the war, much of California, including the Mojave territory, would be turned over to America. This led to many conflicts between Americans and the Natives.

that year, his men were also attacked. During the second fight, the famous frontiersman was slain, along with nine of his men.

By 1850, the Mojave Nation had driven off the European invaders from the west, south, and east. The Mojave were also achieving remarkable victories in their wars against other native peoples. The men of the Quechan-Mojave alliance forced the neighboring Halchidhoma and Kohuana from their homes on the Colorado River. Shoshone-speaking Chemehuevi joined the Mojave in this struggle. As a result, they were given some captured areas on the river to use for their villages.

By the time of the Mexican-American War (1846–1848), the Mojave had established themselves as one of the strongest and most feared nations in western North America. They had successfully combined their traditional lifestyle with the invaders' tools, plants, and animals to produce a unique kind of native society.

The Mojave and the Americans

At the end of the Mexican-American War, the Mojave territory was claimed by the government of the United States. The Native Americans of the Colorado River would soon face a new set of invaders. This time their chief opponents would be the U.S. Army and civilian miners in search of gold. Their efforts would produce a reversal of the Mojave's fortunes.

The first army post on the lower Colorado River was built at Fort Yuma in 1850. Its commander was shocked to discover the Mojave and the Quechan were heavily involved in the native slave trade. They even heard rumors, which turned out to be true, that some of the settlers' children were being held by the Mojave as captive laborers. Government surveyors who were mapping the region also reported that the Native Americans had no fear of the army.

The gold rush that began in the Sierra Nevada brought large numbers of travelers to the Colorado River. Before the end of 1851, large-scale warfare had broken out. Although the Mojave continued to win victories, the numbers of foreigners grew larger. The newcomers who crossed Mojave lands often destroyed precious food resources and created other hardships. In 1852, the Mojave saw the first steamboat move up the river. The people who used the north-south route included European converts to the Church of Latter Day Saints (the Mormons) who were headed for new homes in Utah. The Mojave's territory was becoming a crossroads.

This is a studio portrait of Olive Oatman. She was captured by the Yavapai Indians and sold as a slave to the Mojave. The Mojave treated her well, but tattooed her chin with the mark of a slave.

Despite the newcomers' increasing presence, the members of the Mojave Nation still had faith in their future as a conquering people. In 1857, an expedition of Mojave and Quechan invaded the region to the east along the Gila River. Here, a string of major victories turned into a disaster when the Colorado River people were defeated by the Maricopa and the O'odham. It would be one of the last major battles fought between native nations in North America.

The next year, a force of Mojave attacked a wagon train bound for Sacramento, California. The settlers lost nine men and more than 600 horses and cattle. The travelers were forced to retreat across Arizona

This photo captures a gold mining outfit in California during the gold rush. The desire for gold would draw many newcomers into native lands. Many of these gold mines would ruin the land so precious to the native people.

all the way back to New Mexico. This event made the headlines in newspapers all across America. Colonel William Hoffman organized a force of 700 settlers in San Francisco, who set out from the coast to take revenge. When they arrived on the Colorado River, the Mojave greeted them with friendship, claiming that they had been tricked into fighting by the Hualapai people who lived at the edge of the Grand Canyon. The Americans demanded that a number of Native Americans be surrendered as hostages. A new army base, called Fort Mojave, was established. Soon the fighting was renewed. The Colorado River ran red with human blood.

The decade that began in 1860 brought a fresh round of challenges for the Mojave. A series of horrible epidemics spread through the villages. In 1862, gold was discovered at a place called La Paz in California's Baja peninsula. Large numbers of well-armed miners soon occupied parts of the Mojave homeland. The most important native leader, Yara Tev, wanted to find a peaceful solution to the crisis. He visited the outsiders' cities of Los Angeles and San Francisco. Tev even traveled aboard a ship to the eastern United States, where he met with President Abraham Lincoln. When Tev returned to his people, he argued that they should make

This portrait of Charles Poston was taken in the 1860s. Poston would help bring together many of the leaders of Yuman-speaking tribes, including the Mojave, to develop a reservation.

This 1860s photo shows part of Fort Mojave. The fort would be used by the American military to control the lives of the local Native Americans. The American presence in the Mojave territory would lead to many bloody conflicts.

49

peace. He realized that additional fighting could not end in a Mojave victory.

In 1864, explorer Charles Poston brought together leaders of all of the Yuman-speaking nations to have a conference about the formation of a reservation. The next year, the Colorado River Reservation was opened near Parker, Arizona. The U.S. government expected all the friendly Mojave, Chemehuevi, Cahuilla, Yavapai, Hualapai, and Kawai to move there. Yara Tev was able

This photo, taken in 1863, shows part of the developing Mojave Route at El Dorado Canyon. Routes of travel like this would open the door for settlers to move freely through Native American territories in the West.

to persuade only 500 to 800 of his people to relocate to the new settlement. For the first time, the Mojave Nation was seriously split apart. Homoseh Awahot became the leader of those that rejected cooperation with the government.

Why did some Mojave reject moving to the reservation? They knew that whenever native leaders attempted to make treaties with the American invaders, they were almost always told lies. Many of the proud Mojave could not accept living in these poor conditions, according to rules that were made up by their enemies.

Still, if Native Americans refused to live in the filthy prisons the whites called reservations, they were called dangerous renegades and were often killed without a trial, simply for being Native Americans. The court system almost always protected the invaders at the expense of the natives. Judges even allowed white families to steal native children, who were raised to live as slaves. In 1865, a native boy or girl was worth anywhere from $50 to $100. It was not until 1867 that the United States government began to put an end

This is a painting of Fort Yuma along the Colorado River. Forts like this would seriously impose on the traditional way of life for the Mojave.

to this horrible practice. Adults who did not have any money were often forced by the police to work for food, in order to avoid spending time in jail.

The Mojave who did not live on the reservation were soon deeply divided over the future of their remaining lands. In 1867, a war broke out with their old allies, the Chemehuevi. The Shoshone speakers who had once fought alongside the Mojave were driven from the Colorado River valley. Eventually, some of these Chemehuevi made peace and returned to farm beside the remaining Mojave.

52   This portrait of Mojave people was taken in 1871. The traditional life of the Mojave had gone through great changes over the last 200 years, yet they managed to hold on to many of their traditions in the new century.

The U.S. Army continued its own war of conquest. In 1868, Camp Colorado was founded. Four years later, another outpost was established in the mining town of La Paz. It was a war with few big battles or troop movements. Little by little, the army forced the surviving Native Americans onto reservations.

The fighting finally came to an end in 1890. Officials in Washington, D.C., decided to transform Fort Mojave into a reservation for the remaining Native Americans. Life at Fort Mojave and at the reservation near Parker, Arizona, remained very difficult. Every day the Native Americans faced racism, poverty, and discrimination. Their children were forced to go to schools where they were not allowed to speak their language and were constantly told that their traditions were bad, stupid, or evil. There were shortages of food, and the Native Americans suffered horribly from diseases, with few doctors or nurses available to help them. In 1893, the railroad finally reached the Mojave region. Native craftspeople began to manufacture a few traditional items to sell to travelers. Many people left the reservation to find jobs in the mines, on the trains, and on riverboats. Many of the non-reservation Mojave continued to live in their traditional homeland, in places such as Needles.

Five

The Mojave Today

By 1910, there were barely more than 1,000 Mojave people living on the reservations in Arizona and California. They had gradually adopted more and more of the customs of the newcomers. Most Mojave wore European-style clothing and used the same basic kinds of tools as other Americans. Native ideas about religion and other customs survived, but were rarely seen by outsiders. In less than half a century, the once proud Mojave Nation had been forced into the shadows.

Gradually, attitudes about Native Americans began to change. Mojave men served with distinction in World War I. In 1924, all Native Americans were granted the full benefits of citizenship. Mojave slowly began to win battles over threats to their lands. Finally they started to gain control of their children's educations. Starting in 1930, many government policies even helped, rather than hurt, the native communities. In 1931, the government schools were closed. In 1937, the first modern tribal government was formed at Parker. In 1957, the Fort Mojave Constitution was created.

The twentieth century also had its share of setbacks. In 1935, Hoover Dam was completed, changing the Colorado River forever. The annual floods that brought a new coat of rich mud disappeared. Traditional farming techniques could no longer be

This portrait of Henry Welsh was taken in 1943. Welsh was the chairman of the Mojave tribal council on the Colorado River in the mid-twentieth century. Despite all the challenges, the Mojave Nation has flourished.

56 A nuclear dump site near Needles, California, has become a political hotbed for Native Americans today. Many tribes, including the Mojave, actively protest the dump site. This flag represents the Native Americans' efforts to protect their ancestral lands.

used. Mojave farmers were forced to adopt the same methods as other rural Americans.

Today, thousands of people of Mojave descent live along the Colorado River. The largest single community can be found at the Fort Mojave Reservation. Other Mojave share the Colorado River Indian Reservation at Parker with the Chemehuevi and some Cahuilla. Many other members of the nation live off the reservations.

The Fort Mojave community has a tribal government ruled by a seven-member council. The reservation includes 33,000 acres (13,355 ha) and extends into California, Arizona, and Nevada. The Colorado River Indian Reservation is even larger. It includes more than 280,000 acres (113,312 ha) in California and Arizona.

Both of the reservations are becoming major centers of tourism. The main source of interest is the Colorado River. Non-Indians visit the reservation to go fishing, waterskiing, and boating. The Mojave Nation has modern farms, its own telecommunications company, restaurants, resorts, casinos, and hotels, and near full employment. Mojave leaders are in the forefront of the struggle to preserve what remains of the Colorado River environment. The story of the Mojave Nation provides an example of the ability of a proud people to survive, and even prosper, despite the most extreme challenges.

Timeline

13,000–40,000 years ago	The ancestors of the Mojave nations arrive in North America from Asia.
AD 1	The Mojave begin to farm.
1540–1769	Europeans explore areas near the Mojave Nation. They introduce diseases that are likely to have significantly reduced the size of the population.
1769–1835	The Spanish and Mexican governments establish a chain of missions, towns, and military bases along the California coast and in southern Arizona.
1781	Father Francisco Garcés founds two combined missions and towns on the Colorado River among the Quechan. The Mojave join in the revolt that destroys the settlements.
1826–1848	Increasing numbers of American fur trappers and merchants from New Mexico trade with Indians living in the interior.

1846–1848	The United States conquers California. The Mojave Nation now lives in a region claimed by the United States.
1850	Fort Yuma is founded. Fighting with various Mojave groups will continue through 1890.
1857	Final major campaign against the Maricopa and O'odham. An attack against a pioneer wagon train leads to retaliation by an army of more than 700 settlers.
1862	Gold discovered at La Paz. Miners rush into the Mojave region.
1865	Colorado River Reservation created at Parker, Arizona.
1890	Fort Mojave Reservation created.
1924	All Native Americans made U.S. citizens.
1937	Colorado River Reservation tribal council formed.
1957	Fort Mojave Constitution created.
Present	People of the Mojave Nation remain some of the most active and steadfast activists for Native Americans.

Glossary

alliance (a-LIE-ants) A partnership to further the common interests of a group.

anthropologist (an-thruh-PAH-luh-jist) Researcher who investigates the cultural, social, and physical aspects of human life.

clan (KLAN) A group made up of several families.

epidemic (eh-pih-DEH-mik) Something that affects a large number of individuals within a population or community.

linguistic anthropologist (lin-GWIHS-tik an-thruh-PAH-luh-jist) A researcher of cultures who focuses on the study of languages.

mano (MAH-no) Fist-sized piece of stone that is used to grind nuts and seeds into flour in combination with a metate.

mortar (MOR-tur) A bowl-like device with a circular hole that is used to grind seeds into flour. The Mojave mortars were made out of wood.

metate (me-TOH-tay) Slablike piece of stone with depressions that is used with a mano to grind seeds and nuts into flour.

mission (MI-shun) A system used to spread religious beliefs and goodwill to another country or region.

pestle (PES-tuhl) Cylinder-shaped stone that is used with mortars to grind nuts and seeds into flour.

petroglyph (PEH-truh-glif) Rock art that has designs created using scratching or carving.

prestige (press-TEEJ) A commanding position or position of leadership.

rock art (ROK ART) A form of art that involves scratching, carving, or painting designs or pictures on large rock surfaces.

Resources

BOOKS

Rawl, James J. *Indians of California: The Changing Image.* Norman, OK: University of Oklahoma Press, 1986.

Stanley, Terry. *Digger: The Tragic Fate of the California Indians from the Missions to the Gold Rush.* New York: Crown Publishing/ Random House, 1997.

MUSEUMS

Needles Regional Museum
923 Front Street
Needles, CA 92363
(760) 326-5678
This museum includes exhibits on the nearby Mojave tribe.

WEB SITES

Due to the changing nature of Internet links, The Rosen Publishing Group, Inc., has developed an on-line list of Web sites related to the subject of this book. This site is updated regularly. Please use this link to access the list:

http://www.rosenlinks.com/lnac/moja

Index

63